SMART CAR

Tom Warhol

mc Marshall Cavendish
Benchmark
New York

Published by Marshall Cavendish Benchmark
An imprint of Marshall Cavendish Corporation

Other Marshall Cavendish Offices:
Marshall Cavendish International (Asia) Private Limited, 1 New Industrial Road, Singapore 536196 • Marshall Cavendish International (Thailand) Co Ltd. 253 Asoke, 12th Flr, Sukhumvit 21 Road, Klongtoey Nua, Wattana, Bangkok 10110, Thailand • Marshall Cavendish (Malaysia) Sdn Bhd, Times Subang, Lot 46, Subang Hi-Tech Industrial Park, Batu Tiga, 40000 Shah Alam, Selangor Darul Ehsan, Malaysia

Marshall Cavendish is a trademark of Times Publishing Limited

All websites were available and accurate when this book was sent to press.

Library of Congress Cataloging-in-Publication Data

Warhol, Tom.
Smart car / by Tom Warhol.
p. cm. — (Green cars)
Includes bibliographical references and index.
Summary: "Provides information on the technology used in the Smart Car, and discusses how the green movement is affecting the auto industry"—
Provided by publisher.
ISBN 978-1-60870-012-7
1. Smart automobile — Juvenile literature. 2. Green movement — Juvenile literature. I. Title.
TL215.S58W37 2011
629.222 — dc22
2009035464

Editor: Megan Comerford
Publisher: Michelle Bisson
Art Director: Anahid Hamparian
Series Designer: Daniel Roode

Illustration on pp. 34–35 by Alanna Ranellone

Photo research by Connie Gardner

Cover photo by Bill Pugliano/Stringer/Getty Images

The photographs in this book are used by permission and through the courtesy of: Getty Images: 8, 23, 30, 37, 38, 41; AFP: 13, 16; Ralph Orlowski: 28; Alamy: Oleksly Maksymenko, 40; Ron Kimball/www.kimballstock.com: 10; Corbis: Car Culture, 19; The Image Works: Fuji photos, 24; AP Photo: Kristie Bull: 26.

Printed in Malaysia (T)
135642

Contents

Introduction   4

Chapter 1   Smart Ideas   9

Chapter 2   Car Smarts   17

Chapter 3   Street Smarts   27

Chapter 4   A Smarter Car   31

Vital Stats   40

Glossary   42

Further Information   44

Index   46

Introduction

Most cars in the world run on gasoline, and some cars use more gas than others. Gasoline is made from petroleum, or crude oil, which is a liquid buried deep in the earth. Petroleum formed naturally from the **decomposed** and **compressed** remains of tiny **organisms** that lived millions of years ago. Humans drill deep into the earth to take the oil out.

However, the amount of oil in the world is limited. The more we take out of the ground now, the less there will be in the future, and eventually it will run out. Taking it out of the ground is expensive and damages the **environment**.

Also, when oil and the products made from oil (gasoline, engine oil, heating oil, and diesel fuel) are burned, they give off pollution in the form of gases that damage the **atmosphere**. The carbon dioxide (CO_2) that gasoline-burning engines give off is one of the major causes of **global warming**.

Carbon dioxide is a **greenhouse gas**. Like the glass panes of a greenhouse, the gas traps heat. The build-up of carbon dioxide in the atmosphere, scientists warn, is keeping Earth's heat from escaping into space. As a result, the planet is warming up.

In the United States, about 90 percent of the greenhouse gases we produce is from burning oil, gasoline, and coal. One-third of this comes from the engines that power the vehicles we use to move people and objects around. If we do not stop this global warming, life on Earth could begin to get very uncomfortable.

The problem is not just that temperatures might rise a bit. A warming atmosphere could melt the ice of the Arctic and Antarctic, raise the level of water in the seas, and change the **climate** of many places on Earth. Animals unable to adjust to the new conditions might become extinct (die out). Plants and crops might no longer be able to grow where people need them. Many islands, low-lying countries, and communities along the coasts of all the continents might disappear into the sea.

Doesn't sound so good, does it? These problems are why many people are interested in **alternative fuels** that can power our cars and other engines with less or no pollution.

Now that you know that oil is made from living things that died a long time ago, it should be no surprise that people are making oil from live plants to power their cars. This fuel, called *biodiesel*, can be made from soybean oil, canola oil, sunflowers, and other plants. One form of biodiesel is similar to the vegetable oil used for cooking. Some people gather or buy this used oil from restaurants and use it to power their cars. The engines in these cars have to be modified, or changed, in order to burn this oil correctly.

Another popular way to power cars is with batteries. Modern batteries are being made to be so powerful that some cars use them in combination with gas engines; this system is called *hybrid technology*. Hybrid cars have a gas engine and an electric motor. The electric motor usually takes over when the car runs at low speeds or when it stops.

Many auto engineers are designing electric cars that run only on batteries. Until recently, too many batteries were needed to make this an **efficient** technology. But there have been important advances in battery technology.

Another form of alternative energy for cars is the hydrogen **fuel cell**, which generates power when the hydrogen and oxygen in the fuel cell are combined. If we are to start driving hydrogen-powered cars, however, hydrogen fueling stations would have to be as common along U.S. roads and highways as gas stations are today.

Oil is a limited resource, costs a lot to extract, pollutes the land, air, and water, and forces most countries to rely on the few nations that have a plentiful supply of it. If the world wants to become a cleaner, safer place, developing alternative fuels to power at least some of our vehicles is extremely important.

Most Smart Cars on the roads today run on gasoline. However, because Smart Cars are so lightweight and because the engines are so efficient, they produce far less pollution than most other gasoline-fueled cars. The electric Smart Car will be even more ecofriendly!

Chapter 1
Smart Ideas

How strange it is that in the whole century-long history of the car, there are very few examples of vehicles created specifically to be lightweight, fuel efficient, and easy to park? Even though our cities have become very crowded and polluted, people still drive large cars that use a lot of gas.

This is why the Smart Car took Europe by storm. The Smart Car is much smaller than any other car and it has a unique and colorful design. When the first Smart Car debuted in Europe in 1998, people couldn't help but take notice. These small cars were perfect for Europe's crowded, narrow streets.

◀ **A 2002 Smart Car zips down the road. Because they are so small, Smart Cars are very fuel efficient.**

Smart Cars come with interchangeable plastic body panels. This is what the frame of a Smart Car looks like before the panels are attached.

It took nearly ten years, but American drivers are also starting to warm up to the Smart Car. Only recently have American car buyers started to move away from huge pickup trucks and SUVs in favor of smaller, fuel-efficient vehicles. Many have been motivated by increasing gas prices, but concern about the future of the environment has also played a role in convincing people to take interest in fuel-efficient cars.

Most models of the Smart Car, including the original model, still run on gas rather than alternative fuels. But the Smart Car is one of the most efficient gas-powered cars on the market because it is so small and light. Its size makes it appealing to people, especially people who live in cities. It is also about as long as it is wide, so it can be parked either parallel to the curb or head-in.

Some popular SUVs are as heavy as two or even three Smart Cars and are nearly as wide as the Smart Car is long. Most people don't need a vehicle that big for day-to-day driving.

Though the Smart Car is catching on more slowly in the United States than it did in Europe, it is gaining speed. The Smart Car is particularly successful among people who live in major cities where there is heavy traffic and limited parking.

Fun Facts

The Smart ForTwo is the third most fuel-efficient car in the United States. It beats out many hybrid vehicles. In fact, the Smart ForTwo is the most fuel-efficient non-hybrid car in the country!

A SMART START

The idea for the Smart Car actually started a long time before Smart's current model, the ForTwo, hit the streets. Way back in the early 1970s, Mercedes-Benz (now Daimler AG), a German car manufacturer, decided to try to make a small, fuel-efficient car that was only 7 feet (2.5 meters) long. There are basketball players who are taller than that!

In 1993 Mercedes-Benz joined forces with Nicolas Hayek, the founder of the Swiss watch company Swatch. Swatch had a reputation for making high-quality watches that came in fun, fashionable designs and were reasonably priced. Hayek had first tried collaborating with the car company Volkswagen, but when that venture failed, he partnered with Mercedes-Benz. Hayek brought his ideas for a fashionable, affordable, ultra-urban, two-seater car to the partnership—and to the world of cars.

Smart Cabrios on the assembly line at Smartville in Hambach, France. It takes only eight hours to make a Smart Car from start to finish!

A Smarter Environment

Not only has Smart made a car that saves space, is economical, and pollutes less, the company's production process also helps the planet. Smart keeps its water use and pollution to a minimum, and the cars are made from materials that can be recycled.

The factory reuses heat generated by the machines to heat other parts of the plant. The paints used on the body panels are water-soluble, so they use very little water and no chemical solvents. The company even has a recycling program in Europe for when the cars are too old to run. Smart Car owners can take their cars to Smart-approved recycling facilities, where the cars are taken apart and the materials reused or properly disposed of.

The company's factory, Smartville, in Hambach, France, was also built with the environment in mind. The builders used recycled materials wherever they could, and they didn't use a lot of danger-ous chemical materials typically used in construction. The company also pledged to plant a tree for every Smart Car sold in 2008 and 2009.

Hayek also wanted to make the car fun, like his Swatch watches. The watches have colorful plastic covers that can be easily changed. He wanted Smart Cars to have different-colored door panels that could be swapped, just like his watches.

SMARTVILLE

Though Hayek was creative, he had no experience designing or producing cars. That's exactly what Mercedes-Benz brought to the table. The company had nearly seventy years of experience in the car-manufacturing business.

Swatch and Mercedes-Benz started a third company called Micro Compact Car AG, which was based in Switzerland (later moved to Germany), to start the new line of small cars. A factory was built in Hambach, France, in 1997 to start production of the new cars, called the Swatch Mercedes Art Car, or Smart Car for short. The manufacturing complex was named Smartville.

Mercedes-Benz's design for the Smart Car was more expensive than Hayek wanted it to be, so he sold his share of the partnership. Too bad for him, given how popular the Smart Car has become.

Chapter 2
Car Smarts

Since the Smart ForTwos are gasoline-powered vehicles, their engines are similar to those in many other gas-powered cars. The car is available with three different engines. They are all the same size, at 61 cubic inches (699 cubic centimeters). Putting these engines in the back of the car makes them safer, helps save space, and allows the cars to retain their short and stylish shape.

SMART CHOICES

The basic engine runs on gasoline, and it is available in 64-horsepower (hp) and 71-horsepower versions. Micro Hybrid Drive (MHD), a

◀ **A customized 2009 Smart Car—equipped with WiMAX (wireless communication technology) and an Intel Centrino processor—was on display at the Consumer Electronics Show in Las Vegas, Nevada. It's like a computer on wheels!**

special feature of this engine, senses when the car slows to less than 5 miles per hour (8 kilometers per hour), and it cuts the engine. When the driver takes his or her foot off the brake, the engine starts up again. This saves gasoline and puts less carbon dioxide into the air.

The turbo engine gives the car a boost to 84 horsepower, letting the car reach a maximum speed of 90 miles per hour (145 km/h). The special BRABUS edition has a more powerful 98-horsepower turbo gas engine.

The 45-horsepower diesel engine for the Smart ForTwo is also turbocharged. Though it is not available in the United States, it is one of the most fuel-efficient cars on the world market. A Smart ForTwo Diesel gets an estimated 84 miles per gallon (36 kilometers per liter) and produces 23 percent fewer carbon dioxide emissions than a regular gasoline engine.

All models are built using the company's tridion safety cell. The superstrong shell of the car is made of three layers of steel, and it is designed to prevent the car from crushing its passengers during an accident. In the newer models, the tridion cell shows through the outer layer of the car. The tridion cell is painted in colors that contrast with the Smart Car's body using powder paints, which are much more environmentally friendly than other car paints.

This cutaway of a Smart ForTwo makes it easy to see the tridion safety cell.

The body panels, including the doors, fit into the frame of the safety cell and are easily removable. Smart makes them in different colors from scratch-resistant, recycled plastic. The panels also resist denting from small impacts.

At 8 feet 10 inches long (2.7 m), the Smart Car's small size makes it easy to fit into any parking space. It can even be parked head-on into parallel-parking spaces. However, only some countries allow this kind of parking. The United States and Germany have banned it.

SAFETY FIRST

Although Mercedes-Benz started designing a mini car in the early 1970s at their facility in Irvine, California, it wasn't until the early 1990s that the first concept cars premiered at car shows. It took that long for engineers and designers to make the car safe enough to drive. They needed to be sure that such a small car could stand up to impacts with larger vehicles.

The design they eventually came up with was the tridion safety cell, which was part of the first concept Smart Cars, the Eco Sprinter and the Eco Speedster, that were displayed at car shows in 1993.

The next-generation concept car in the Smart line was the 1996 Atlanta show car. This brightly colored car had no doors so people at the show could get a better sense of the size of the car's interior.

Later that same year, the Paris show car was the first model to showcase both concepts that have become trademarks of the Smart brand: the tridion safety cell and the interchangeable body panels.

The Frankfurt Motor Show concept car, called the City-Coupe Fashion Victim, had a design similar to that of current Smart Cars. It was the first model to have the safety cell painted a contrasting color to the car's body panels.

The first production model, the Smart City-Coupe, was rolled out in 1998 in five European countries. The company focused its marketing strategy on the spacious interior despite the small exterior and a very small **turning radius**. The car featured a 37-cubic-inch (599 cc) turbo engine and a six-speed automatic transmission, with an electronic speed lock that kept the car from going more than 70 miles per hour (113 km/h). But best of all was the car's excellent **fuel economy**, which meant it saved its drivers money.

The extra time engineers took to make sure this first consumer model was safe paid off. Several independent safety companies tested the Smart City-Coupe. Their results showed that because of the tridion safety shell, the Smart Car was one of the sturdiest and safest cars made.

Fun Facts

British pop star Robbie Williams was the first person to order a Crossblade, and Smart sponsored the singer's 2002 European tour. He specifically requested car number 0008. The first of the limited edition, number 0001, was auctioned off. The money from the winning bid went to Williams's own charity to help fight poverty. The singer went on to help promote the company's ForFour.

EARLY TRIES

Smart introduced its sports-car concept car in 1999. The Smart Roadster featured a slick design and a modified front axle. It had the same engine as the City-Coupe. But the Roadster didn't have the electronic lock on its speed that the City-Coupe did, so the Roadster could reach faster speeds. The Smart Roadster went into production between 2003 and 2005, but the company stopped making them because they weren't selling well.

The Crossblade started as a concept car in 2001 and was produced as a limited edition. Only 2,000 vehicles were made. It was truly a never-before-seen car—no doors, no roof, and no windshield. The interior was waterproof and had holes in the floor to drain rainwater. A **rollbar** was included as a safety feature.

The Tridion 4, Smart's first four-passenger car, was introduced in 2001 and went into production as the ForFour in 2004. Despite the car's increased interior space and five-door design, it measured only 12 feet (3.65 m) in length. Many people thought this car was too far away from Smart's original idea for a small, stylish, and efficient city car. Very few ForFours were sold. Smart discontinued the line in 2006.

The Smart Roadster Coupe combined the design of a traditional sports car with the uniqueness of the Smart Car.

The Crosstown—the car that most closely resembled the ForTwo—debuted in 2005 as a concept car, but it never went into production. It automatically switched between a gas-powered motor and an electric motor for peak efficiency. A hybrid four-wheel-drive transmission, a convertible top, and a removable windshield made it the most versatile Smart Car yet.

The Crossblade was on display at the 2001 Tokyo Motor Show in Japan. Without a windshield or a roof, it was not a practical car.

FORTWO FOR YOU

In 1998 Daimler-Benz merged with the U.S.-based Chrysler Corporation to become DaimlerChrysler. By this point Daimler had almost closed the Smart factories as a result of poor sales. Fortunately, the company refocused their efforts and got rid of all of their other car models except for one. They went back to work on the original design for the City-Coupe, made the car a little bigger, improved it's look and it's safety features, renamed it the ForTwo, and released it in 2006.

Finally, in 2006 Smart unveiled the new version of the Smart For-Two, which had increased efficiency, agility, comfort, and safety. The car is slightly longer than the original model. It was released to the public in spring 2007. The Smart ForTwo features an automated manual transmission, which means it has both automatic and manual modes. The driver can choose to change gears in manual mode by moving the gearshift, or in automatic mode by just tapping the top of the gearshift.

The new design was a success, and the Smart ForTwo is now sold in thirty-eight countries, including the United States.

Chapter 3
Street Smarts

The original production model, the Smart City-Coupe, quickly became a popular car because of its fun, original look, great gas mileage, and safe design.

However, Smart didn't stop there. They kept improving the car, gradually increasing the engine size from the original 37-cubic-inch (599 cc) to 43-cubic-inch (698 cc) and eventually to the current 61-cubic-inch (999 cc) engine.

Smart also added their unique Electronic Stability Program (esp®) package to the car. The package included the Anti-Lock Braking System, Brake Assist, Hill Start Assist, and other innovations to make the car even more stable and easy to handle.

◀ **The bright red body panels made the Smart ForTwo Passion cabriolet stand out at the 2008 New York Auto Show.**

Smart Car

This tower of Smart Cars is actually a parking garage! Each of the seven levels has space for four Smart Cars. There is an elevator system that brings the cars to the parking spots.

And finally, with the addition of several new models to the line, including the Roadster and the ForFour, Smart decided to rename the two-seater car to fit this new line. Thus, the Smart ForTwo was born, and it quickly outsold all of its siblings.

FORTWO TIMES FOUR

With this success came the addition of several models to the ForTwo line. In Europe, Smart ForTwos are available in four different models: Pure, which is the basic version; the Pulse, which has a sportier look and feel; the Passion, a more elegant and cushy car for those who want to be environmentally conscious and stylish; and the BRABUS, with a more powerful engine and sportier interior. All models except the economical Pure have sunroofs.

The interchangeable plastic body panels are made of recycled materials and are available in six colors: rally red, deep black, crystal white, blue metallic, silver metallic, and gray metallic.

The Smart ForTwo Pulse, Passion, and BRABUS models each come with a sunroof in the coupe style or a convertible top in the sportier cabriolet style. As the most inexpensive convertible on the market, the cabriolets were extremely popular when they were first released.

In the United States, only the Pure, Passion, and BRABUS versions are available, and they come with a 70-horsepower engine. Like the European versions, both the Passion and the BRABUS are available as either a coupe or cabriolet.

Chapter 4
A Smarter Car

Even though the models in the line of Smart Cars are impressively ecofriendly, engineers at Smart are working to make them even greener. The company has developed an all-electric car, called the ForTwo ED (Electric Drive), that is being tested in Europe. The company hopes to launch a pilot program in U.S. cities in late 2010. Smart plans to begin producing the ForTwo ED in 2012.

◀ **A Smart ED on display at the 2008 Paris Motor Show in France.**

Smart Trials

In London, England, one hundred Smart electric cars have been in use since 2007, many of them by the London police. These ForTwo ED models can reach a maximum speed of 70 miles per hour (113 km/h) and have a range of 72 miles (116 km). Smart also introduced an improved model into the Paris market in 2008 with an extended range of 150 miles (241 km).

Starting in 2010, another one hundred cars will be on the streets in Berlin, Germany, where the company has also started a network of public charging stations so people can charge their cars on the go. Plans are afoot to test the cars in Rome, Milan, and Pisa in Italy as well. The company expects to start marketing the Smart ED in limited numbers in select cities in the United States in late 2010.

THINK ELECTRIC!

The first ForTwo ED models used a sodium-nickel chloride battery to power the electric motor. However, advances in ED technology have resulted in Smart's switch to a lithium-ion battery. This is the same kind of battery used in most hybrid vehicles. It was made standard in all Smart EDs in late 2009.

The car's battery pack can be charged from a 220-volt electrical outlet, the same type used for appliances like washers and dryers. A full charge takes about eight hours. The battery also recharges when the driver applies the brakes—energy is created by the **friction** of the brakes. This is called regenerative braking. ForTwo ED drivers in London who drive about 30 miles (50 km) each day can fully recharge the car's battery in three to four hours.

The best part of all is that the Smart electric car releases zero emissions, so it is one of the cleanest, greenest cars ever produced.

This electric technology is important, and it may be where many car companies turn for their new car designs in the future. It emits no pollution, runs quietly, and can be charged easily and inexpensively. Several cities in Europe, and a few in the United States, have even set up charging stations. These are public electric outlets specifically for charging electric or plug-in hybrid vehicles.

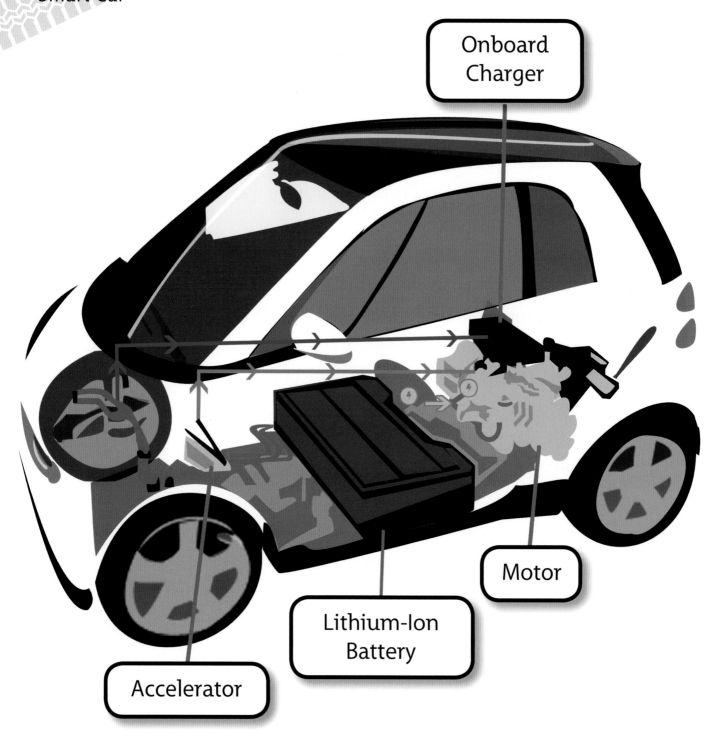

Onboard Charger

Motor

Lithium-Ion Battery

Accelerator

Smart Car ED

In the Smart Car ED, the lithium-ion battery will power the electric motor, which will respond to the driver's pressure on the accelerator. When the driver applies the brakes it creates energy. That energy will be stored onboard to extend the battery charge.

Key

— Connecting Wires

⚡ Electric Power

— Energy from braking is stored in the charger

— Signal from the accelerator to the motor

ALTERNATIVE FUELS

Smart is not the only company to build cars that run on electricity. Toyota and Honda, makers of the popular Prius and Insight hybrids, have both put tremendous effort into developing drivable electric cars.

Some hybrids, including the Prius, can be altered to run on only electric power. These are called plug-in electric vehicles, or PHEVs for short, and they can be plugged into a wall outlet to recharge the battery.

Some companies have been experimenting with other alternative fuels, including hydrogen. In a hydrogen-powered car, hydrogen and oxygen react to produce electricity. That electricity powers the motor, which makes the car run. Some companies have developed engines in which hydrogen is burned, similar to the way gasoline is burned in a gas-powered car.

Though hydrogen cars are technologically possible, they are not practical. In order to drive a hydrogen car, there would first have to be hydrogen-fueling stations. Furthermore, engineers still haven't figured out a way for a vehicle to carry enough hydrogen to enable to travel long distances without refueling.

A Smarter Car

The Smart ED is easy to charge. There is a door over the rear tire for the plug, just like a regular car has a door for the gas pump.

Smart Car

A Smart Car parked in front of the entrance to a Smart dealership in Michigan.

SMART FUTURE

The fact that there are so many designs for cars running on cleaner, alternative fuels means that people are and will always be looking for new and better ideas for automobile technology. Although cars will probably still run on gas for a long time, having more and more cars on the road that use alternative fuels means that we won't have to pollute Earth so much.

Having several different technologies going at once means that if one type of fuel or technology becomes scarce or has problems, we can switch to other types more easily. Smart Cars are fun to drive, come in bright colors, have interchangeable parts, are very safe, and are better for the environment, so Smart Cars really are smart!

Vital Stats

2009 SMART FORTWO

Power: 70 hp

Curb Weight: 1,808 lbs (820 kg)

Seats: 2

Top Speed: 90 mph (145 km/h)

0–60 mph (0–97 km/h): 12.8 seconds

Average Fuel Economy: 37 mpg (16 km/l)

2009 SMART FORTWO ED

Battery type: lithium-ion

Curb Weight: 2,228 lbs (1,011 kg)

Seats: 2

Top Speed: 70 mph (113 km/h)

0–60 mph (0–97 km/h): 13 seconds

Battery Life: 100 miles (160 km)

Recharge Time: 2–4 hours

Glossary

alternative fuels   Substances, other than gasoline and other petroleum products, that can be used to power engines.

atmosphere   The air surrounding Earth.

climate   The average weather of a place over many years.

compressed   Squeezed together; in the case of the life-forms that became oil, they were pressed together over millions of years by layers of rock and soil.

decomposed   Broken down into parts or basic elements; when plants or animals die, because of time, weather, and the action of insects and bacteria, they are broken down.

efficient   To function without much waste or unnecessary effort.

environment   The rock, soil, air, and water that sustains all life, as well as the life-forms they sustain.

friction   The force, in the form of heat, that is generated when two solid objects come into contact with each other.

fuel cell   A device that changes a chemical fuel, such as hydrogen, into electrical energy, which can power a vehicle.

fuel economy	A measure of how efficient a car is, based on how much fuel it uses; given in miles per gallon (mpg).
global warming	An increase in Earth's average yearly temperature that is believed to be caused by pollution and that results in climate changes.
greenhouse gas	A gas, such as carbon dioxide, that contributes to global warming
organisms	Living things.
rollbar	A strong, U-shaped metal bar that is mounted on a vehicle in place of or as part of the roof to protect the passengers in case the vehicle rolls over.
turning radius	The size of the smallest circular turn that a vehicle can make.
solvents	Liquid substances that are used to clean or thin out paints. Some solvents are very toxic, or poisonous.
water-soluble	Able to be dissolved in water.

Further Information

BOOKS

Bearce, Stephanie. *Tell Your Parents All about Electric and Hybrid Cars.* Hockessin, DE: Mitchell Lane Publishers, 2009.

Famighetti, Robert. *How Do Hybrid Cars Work?* Science in the Real World. New York: Chelsea House, 2009.

Juettner, Bonnie. *Hybrid Cars.* Chicago, IL: Norwood House Press, 2009.

Welsbacher, Anne. *Earth-Friendly Design.* Saving Our Living Earth. New York: Lerner, 2008.

WEBSITES

Energy Kids, website run by the Energy Information Administration, provides information about energy use in the United States.
http://tonto.eia.doe.gov/kids/

Energy Quest is the California Energy Commission's guide to alternative fuel vehicles. There is information on cars that run on gasoline, hydrogen, electricity, and biodiesel, as well as links to sources with more information.
www.energyquest.ca.gov/transportation/

Science News for Kids's article "Ready, Unplug, Drive" has lots of information about plug-in and electric cars.
www.sciencenewsforkids.org/articles/20081029/Feature1.asp

Smart USA is the official Smart Car website for the United States. You can find information about the safety features, the available models, and Smart's participation in the American Forests' Global ReLeaf campaign.
www.smartusa.com

Index

The page numbers in **boldface** are photographs, illustrations, or diagrams.

A
alternative fuels, 5, 39
    biodiesel, 5–6
    electric motors, 31, 33
    hydrogen cars, 36
    hydrogen fuel cells, 7
    Smart ForTwo ED, 31, 32, 33,
        34–35, 37

B
batteries, 6, 32, 33, 41
biodiesel, 5–6
body panels, **10**, 15, 20, **26**, 29
brakes, 27, 33, 35

C
carbon dioxide (CO_2), 4, 18
charging, Smart ForTwo ED, 33, **37**
charging stations, 32, 33
cities, Smart Cars and, 9
City-Coupe Fashion Victim concept
    car, 21

climate change, 4–5
concept cars, 20, 21, 22, 24
convertibles, **16**, **26**, 29
Crossblade, 22, **24**
Crosstown, 24

D
DaimlerChrysler, 25
development of the Smart Car, 12,
    15, 20, 21
diesel engines, 18

E
Eco Speedster, 20
Eco Sprinter, 20
electric cars, 31, **34–35**, 36. *See also*
    Smart ForTwo ED
electric motors, 6, 33
Electronic Stability Program, 27
emissions, Smart ForTwo ED, 33
energy independence, alternative
    fuels and, 7
engines, 6, 17–18, 21, 27, 33
environmental issues, 4–5, 11, 14,
    36, 39
Europe, Smart Cars in, 9, 32

Index

F
fossil fuels, 4, 5
fuel efficiency, 11, 12, 18, 21, 40, 41

G
gasoline, 4, 11
gasoline engines, 17
global warming, 4–5
greenhouse gases, 4–5

H
Hayek, Nicolas, 12, 15
Honda Insight, 36
hybrid technologies, 6, 17–18, 24, 36
hydrogen cars, 7, 36
hydrogen fuel cells, 7

L
lithium-ion batteries, 32, 33, **34–35**, 41

M
manufacturing, **10**, **13**, 14, 15
Mercedes-Benz, 12, 15, 20
Micro Compact Car AG, 15
Micro Hybrid Drive (MHD) engine, 17–18

P
parking, 9, 11, 20, **28**
plug-in electric vehicle (PHEV), 36
pollution, 4, 7, 14
popularity, 9, 11, 25

R
range, Smart ForTwo ED, 32, 33
rear view, **38**
recycling, of Smart Cars, 14

S
safety, 18, 20–21
sea levels, global warming and, 5
size, automobiles and, 11, 20, 40, 41
Smart City-Coupe, 21, 25, 27, 29
Smart ForFour, 23, 29
Smart ForTwo, **8**, 12, **13**, **16**, 25, 29, **40**
Smart ForTwo BRABUS, 29
Smart ForTwo ED, **30**, 31, 32, 33, **34–35**, **37**, **41**
Smart ForTwo Passion, **26**, 29
Smart ForTwo Pulse, 29
Smart ForTwo Pure, 29
Smart Roadster Coupe, 22, **23**, 29
Smartville (factory), **13**, 14, 15
speeds, 21, 22, 32, 40, 41
SUVs, 11
Swatch, 12, 15

T
transmissions, 25, 33
Tridion 4, 23
tridion safety cell, **10**, 18, **19**, 20
Toyota Prius, 36
turbo engines, 18

U
United States, Smart Cars in, 11, 12, 20, 25, 29, 32

V
Volkswagen, 12

W
Williams, Robbie, 22

About the Author

Tom Warhol has written several books, including *Eagles*, *Hawks*, and *Owls* in the AnimalWays series and the six-volume series Biomes of Earth for Marshall Cavendish Benchmark. He is also a naturalist and photographer with an interest in green technology and alternative energy.